LEVERAGING
— YOUR —
LEADERSHIP
STYLE

WORKBOOK

LEVERAGING
— YOUR —
LEADERSHIP
STYLE

WORKBOOK

Maximize Your Influence by Discovering the Leader Within

John Jackson and Lorraine Bossé-Smith

Abingdon Press
Nashville

LEVERAGING YOUR LEADERSHIP STYLE WORKBOOK
MAXIMIZE YOUR INFLUENCE BY DISCOVERING THE LEADER WITHIN
Copyright © 2008 by Lorraine Bossé-Smith and John Jackson

This book is printed on acid-free paper.

ISBN 978-0-687-65059-0

08 09 10 11 12 13 14 15 16 17—10 9 8 7 6 5 4 3 2 1
MANUFACTURED IN THE UNITED STATES OF AMERICA

We would like to dedicate this book to YOU!
No matter what your role or title,
you *will* make a difference in the lives of others!

Acknowledgments

Thank you, Team Abingdon! Everyone has been so professional, kind, and encouraging to work with. In particular, I appreciate John Kutsko's support and belief in John and me. Together, we'll impact lives— Deo Valente!

To Ron Penland, Jim Canfield, and all others at Renaissance Executive Forums, thank you for helping me get to the next level.

—*Lorraine Bossé-Smith*

The writing of a book has been compared by some to childbirth. While I can't attest to that and I'm sure that the notion would receive heated debate by others, I know that it is a long and arduous process. The entire team at Abingdon has been amazing to work with, and I join Lorraine in thanking John and Jessica in particular for their support. Thanks also to all the leaders who have shaped me on my leadership journey.

—*Dr. John Jackson*

Contents

INTRODUCTION
Transform Your Leadership

R eady to take a road trip? I'm assuming by now that you have read the book, *Leveraging Your Leadership Style*, and that now you want to take some more practical steps to equip yourself and your team members. In some of the chapters that I (John) write, I'll be using the analogy of a road trip. I grew up in a family that took long road trips (counted in days, not miles!). I knew the privilege and the pain of taking a road trip with a family full of different kinds of travelers, every one of which is now a different kind of leader. I complained the entire length of the trips, but when I arrived at adulthood, those road trips were some of my fondest memories (thanks, Dad and Mom!).

You have taken your own road trips in the course of your life. Whether or not these trips have been in a car or in a variety of different life experiences in corporate and personal situations, you have learned about leadership on your journey. You may not think of yourself as a leader, but the truth is that you are. In fact, here is what I know: you actually know more about leadership than you think you know. Our definition of leadership is "leveraging influence in the context of healthy relationships," and you have been exercising leadership whether you know it or not!

You are a person of influence and a leader. You influence others and want to be more effective with your leadership and your relationships. You'll get the most help from this workbook if you go slowly. I know that many of you are "Type A" driven leaders (welcome—we are too!), and you'll want to speed through the exercises. Resist the urge! Yes, I know, I'm probably risking your emotional equilibrium, but I believe you can do it. Instead of hydroplaning over the surface of the materials, take your time to absorb the materials and then share them with your key team members. Work the materials into the context of your team building time rather than just "doing" the materials as an assignment.

The goal of this workbook is to give you very practical tools so that you can be a better leader and equip your team to be a better team. Commanders, you *will* finish this workbook (probably first!). Coaches, you can enjoy these pages with your team, and you'll make it fun! Counselors, you

1

will be enriched by the process, and you can add value to each of your team members through the process. Conductors, you will be efficient and effective throughout the process, and you will cross the finish line! So, fasten your seatbelt and start your engines. We're ready to roll!

—Dr. John Jackson

The movie *The Transformers* is a live-action (computer-enhanced, of course) version of a decades-old cartoon in which semi-tractor-trailer trucks and other vehicles change and become something even more powerful. The movie introduces us to good and evil transformers, all with their own objectives. I believe the same is true of leaders: in each of us, we have something great waiting to explode! In every one of us is also the ability to do good or bad with what we have inside. All one needs to do is read the paper or watch the news to discover plenty of folks in both camps. Our history books are full of amazing leaders who founded the very country we live in today. On the same pages are corrupt and misguided leaders who have attempted to destroy society as we know it.

Leveraging Your Leadership Style and this companion workbook are not books of psychology but rather insights into the behaviors or personality temperaments that we all have been given. What we do with them is our choice, and I'm very glad that you have decided to put your gifts and talents to good use! As leaders, no matter what our role or title, we have a responsibility to others. And great leadership starts within.

Just like the Transformers toys or characters from the movie, we must control what comes out to the public. We all have strengths that, when pushed to an extreme, can become weaknesses or negative traits. The more we know about ourselves, the better we can lead. Couple this with a ferocious appetite to understand others, and you have the makings of a remarkable leader . . . one that people follow because of who you are, not because of your position.

I truly believe that any person in leadership desires such a healthy leader-follower relationship deep down inside. Some may have forgotten why they got into leadership, falling prey to worldly/trendy/false views. Others may doubt that such a bond can be formed. Have hope! Building bridges and creating stronger teams is what *Leveraging Your Leadership Style* is all about. And with this workbook, you will learn how to apply the strategies discussed in specific situations. Consider this practice, and practice makes perfect.

How do professional tennis players get on the circuit? By playing tennis . . . a lot! They didn't just show up one day. Instead, they hit a bazillion tennis balls behind the scenes. By the time you and I see them on television, they are experts. You have been exposed to some new ideas on leadership and how your particular style influences others. Now it is your turn to hit a few balls, practice your serve, and get in the game of leading with style.

You will need a copy of *Leveraging Your Leadership Style* and will want to take the assessment. I highly encourage you to read through the chapter that corresponds to your particular style before diving into the workbook. This workbook will complement what you have learned and take it to the next level by providing you with very realistic case studies. You will have the opportunity to think and determine how you would respond to these hypothetical dilemmas, all in the safety of this book. This isn't about winning and conquering your opponent, though; it is about becoming a better leader, one to be proud of in years to come.

—*Lorraine Bossé-Smith*

CHAPTER ONE
Building Bridges

Leveraging Your Leadership Style is all about positive and proactive influence in the context of healthy relationships. What that means in practical terms is that leaders have to learn to operate using their own leadership style in relationship (and sometimes in tension!) with everyone else on their team. Marcus Buckingham, author of *First Break All the Rules*, suggests that leaders need to understand several different aspects of those they work with:

Striving Talents, Thinking Talents, and Relating Talents

Striving talents explain the *why* of a person. They explain *why* we get out of bed every day, *why* we are motivated to push and push just that little bit harder.

Thinking talents explain the *how* of a person. They explain *how* we think, *how* we weigh alternatives, *how* we come to decisions.

Relating talents explain the *who* of a person. They explain *whom* we trust, *whom* we build relationships with, *whom* we confront and *whom* we ignore.[1]

As you think about the striving, thinking, and relating talents of each of your team members, you will no doubt begin to reference our four leadership styles: Commander, Coach, Counselor, and Conductor. Each of the leadership styles has a different approach to being on the team and leading the team. For you as team leader or team participant, your challenge is to understand the "why," the "how," and the "who" of people's participation in and leadership of teams. The more you can understand yourself and others as well as the interaction between them, the more you'll leverage your leadership! This workbook will help you put into real-life practice the principles we described in the *Leveraging Your Leadership Style* book itself.

A Trip down Memory Lane

When I was a kid, my parents never liked owning a home. In fact, they have only ever owned one home. It had a pool and was really nice. But it took a lot of work, and it kept them from the one thing they loved for us to do together . . . travel! I can't tell you how many "road trips" we took when I was a kid. In fact, one of the luxuries of my dad's 24-7 job was that we got three to four weeks of vacation every year. So as a kid, I learned to count vacations not in light of days gone from home, but in miles traveled! I complained terribly (mostly about riding in a cramped backseat with my three siblings), but as an adult, those trip memories are some of my greatest childhood treasures.

So I thought we'd take a short road trip together. I've become convinced that every team and every leader are a little bit like drivers and passengers on the road trips of my childhood. In fact, each trip is different based on what the driver is like. Think about the teams you serve on or perhaps the teams you lead. Do any of these road trip descriptions sound familiar to you?

Road Trip!

Road Trips with a Commander: Commanders are about achieving the goal. Finishing the journey is the most important thing. Well, not exactly. Finishing the trip is close to being the *only* thing! Getting there ahead of schedule, ahead of others and ahead of projected personal calculations are the primary objectives. If you are a passenger with a Commander, **do not** drink any water. Bathroom stops are highly discouraged! Side trips will only happen for this group if they are a shortcut! A passenger traveling with a Commander driver will finish the journey before anyone else. But, unless this group is full of Commanders, it is probably not the happiest carload of people.

Road Trips with a Coach: Coaches are about the team. Making sure that all the passengers in the vehicle are happy with each other is a key concern. Coaches develop a game plan that will help them complete the journey, but they are also very concerned that the team members are fulfilled on the journey. If you are a passenger with a Coach, be prepared for frequent rest stops to make sure everyone is "on-board." In fact, a side trip might even happen if **everyone** agrees that it would be fun. Passengers traveling with good Coach drivers will finish the journey—**together**.

Road Trips with a Counselor: Counselors are about the health of the individual. Counselors want to know that each person is fulfilled, living a life of purpose and meaning and also fulfilling their potential. Taking a road trip with a Counselor? Expect frequent probing, supportive, and penetrating questions about how you are experiencing the journey. Side trips for this group could happen if the driver is convinced that it would be personally enriching to each passenger. You will probably arrive at your destination later than most, but you will have a great deal more understanding of the journey you've traveled.

Road Trips with a Conductor: Conductors are about the strategy and the structure of the trip. Conductors will want to ensure that the trip is well planned, researched, and executed. Mileage markers (and bathroom stops!) will be known in advance and calculated. Conductors will start later than others because of the preparation time involved, but the overall efficiency of the trip should far surpass any other driving type; and if it doesn't, expect pressure! Passengers traveling with Conductors can rightly expect an on-time arrival with the most direct route planned in advance. Don't expect time for side trips on this bus; they don't fit into the efficient schedule the Conductor has planned.

So, have you taken a road trip with one of these drivers? Have you *been* one of these drivers? I hope you are smiling . . . because I'll bet you recognize yourself in these drivers. I know I do (and I'm sure my poor family recognizes me as well)! Self-awareness is a key to leadership.

Let's Hit the Road

Growing and developing your work teams is a little bit like taking a road trip. Sometimes we can get cranky with our fellow passengers under ordinary circumstances; and if your team members have widely different styles, your road trip may feel more like crossing the plains in a covered wagon! You'll have to think through what kind of driver you are and what kind of passengers you have in your car. Spend a moment now and think that one through.

1. What kind of driver are *you* on a road trip? What is the highest value for you when you are taking a long journey?

_____

_____

2. Pretend you are taking your family of four on a 500-mile road trip in your family car. How would you go about preparing for the trip? What would the trip be like for your passengers?

_____

_____

_____

3. Think for a moment about your team. Do they think just like you? Or are you often surprised (annoyed?) when they appear to have different values or priorities than you do? See if you can identify what type of driver each member of your primary team would be if they were taking a road trip.

_____

_____

_____

Making the Trip Together

In our history books, the true heroes and exceptional leaders did not make decisions from an ivory tower. Rather, they were in the trenches, alongside their troops. Consider giving your team this road trip exercise during a staff meeting or corporate retreat. Have everyone think about the above questions and then share what his or her potential road trip was like. Better yet, break the ice by having your team bring in and share a photo of their favorite road trip! Just as my family trips (and subsequent trips as an adult) taught me a great deal about others and myself, this exercise can really shed some light (and laughter) on your team.

I encourage you as a leader to take time for some short road trips for your team—especially your top management or executive staff. The more time you spend together, the stronger the bridge will be between you. Now, that is leveraging your leadership style!

CHAPTER TWO
Create Stronger Relationships

I hope you enjoyed John's road trip analogy in chapter 1! For those who are fast-paced, you may want to skip right to the chapter focusing on your particular leadership style. However, if you are interested in understanding why it is so critical for you and your business to build stronger relationships, we invite you to join us for this chapter. Those who appreciate facts and statistics will definitely want to absorb this information. Research offers many insights into the value of relationships in organizations and what needs to be done in order to grow businesses beyond today.

We already know that leadership is all about relationships. And according to the American Management Association, the future of business depends upon them.[1] With the aging of the population and a new breed of workers, businesses must respond correctly or we all could be in a world of hurt. Down to an interpersonal level, leaders need to pay attention to the changes in the marketplace in order to make necessary adaptations.

Job dissatisfaction is at an all-time high. AMA reports that only 29 percent of workers feel engaged on the job. Workers are no longer staying put and suffering through a poor work environment.[2] Mark Sanborn, author of the best-selling book, *The Fred Factor*, states that the number one reason why employees leave is a lack of appreciation.[3] Couple that with an upcoming shortage of people able to work (due to the retirement of baby boomers), and we had better pay attention and get more serious about the relationships we have with our employees.

I recently heard a story of a man who called an emergency meeting with his management staff to do something about the company's high turnover. He proposed that new incentives and benefits be introduced to entice employees to stay. A brave executive addressed the president and asked, "Sir, have you ever considered that *we* might be part of the problem?" You may have heard it said before: "People don't leave jobs; they leave bosses." Ouch! Although it can sting, as leaders we need to acknowledge and accept responsibility. The way we communicate, direct, coach, counsel, and conduct ourselves does impact the entire organization.

If things aren't going as we would like, we need to look inward first before blaming processes. Certainly, all systems can be evaluated and possibly improved, but sometimes the problem lies within.

We're Not in Kansas Anymore!

The 2000 Bureau of Labor Statistics estimated that by the year 2008 our country would have 5 to 6.2 million more jobs than people able to fill them, and they were right! Businesses are already feeling the crunch, having difficulty recruiting and retaining top talent.[4] As leaders, we have to create stronger relationships and engage employees; money only goes so far as a motivator. Work environment is essential. Judith Glaser, author of *Creating WE: Change I-Thinking to We-Thinking & Build a Healthy, Thriving Organization*, points out that people want a place to develop and flourish.[5] Employees want to be valued for their contributions and recognized for meeting those audacious goals management can set. In short, they want to be allowed to succeed. As leaders, we must provide that atmosphere. How? By knowing what people want.

Every one of your employees and customers has a unique set of issues and needs for you to consider. Caring enough to *know* your people will reduce your turnover and increase job satisfaction. By motivating, managing, encouraging and rewarding people based upon their unique preferences, you will save yourself a lot of heartache . . . and money.

The president of a company I worked for many years ago impressed me so that I still remember it. He had run the company for twenty-five-plus years. We were at a trade show specific to our industry, and as he walked the floor, he greeted each and every person by his or her first name. This alone was amazing, given that he was greeting hundreds of people, but what really got me was how he remembered what was going on in their lives. He'd ask how their son was doing in college or if they recovered from the surgery they had last year. He truly took an interest in his customers, and had a gift for retaining the details of their lives—a gift that we don't all have. However, we can all get to know the people on our team intimately.

> *People don't care about how much you know*
> *until they know how much you care.*
>
> —Anonymous

Bobby Bowden, head football coach for the Florida State Seminoles, lists compassion right alongside integrity and courage as key virtues of great leaders. According to Bowden, it is critical to not only be honest with your people and stand up for what you believe in but to have a deep love for those working under you.[6]

I (Lorraine) have worked for numerous nonprofit organizations in my corporate career. Salaries are typically lower and the workload heavier than in other jobs. Yet, as a leader, I was able to build strong teams of employees who were satisfied and engaged. What I couldn't give them in monetary rewards I gave them in encouragement, support, and career enhancement. Never underestimate what training or a seminar can do for an employee. Besides improving their job skills, personnel often feel valued and appreciated. The underlying message they hear is clear: "They wouldn't invest in a deadbeat employee . . . I must matter."

Make a Difference

I believe everyone wants to matter and to make a difference, regardless of his or her position. I also think the aging of our country's workforce is going to force everyone to lead better and be more creative with how they motivate, reward, and retain top talent. That's a good thing! Throwing money at problems never really solves them—it just hides them or delays the inevitable. As leaders, we must throw ourselves in, roll up our sleeves, and get relational.

Getting Serious

OK, so maybe you haven't done an exceptional job of building up your team up until now. Then start today. John Maxwell, leadership guru, reminds us that yesterday ended last night. He encourages us not to "overexaggerate yesterday or underestimate today because the one thing we have is today."[7] We can't change our past decisions, but we can learn from them. What is incredible about doing the right things from this point forward is that you will dramatically change tomorrow. The future success of your business will be influenced by what you do today. Think for a moment about these questions:

1. How well do you know your employees?

_____

_____

_____

2. What could you do to get to know them better and to show your interest in their lives?

_____

_____

_____

3. Besides money, how could you show your employees that they matter to you?

_____

_____

_____

> *If people are coming to work excited . . . if they're making mistakes freely and fearlessly . . . if they're having fun . . . if they're concentrating on doing things rather than preparing reports and going to meetings—then somewhere, you have a leader.*
> —*Robert Townsend*[8]

Begin looking at your employees as associates or partners. They aren't showing up to serve you but rather to work alongside of you to achieve a common goal. If you have done your job right, you have cast the vision. And this vision is what brings them back day after day. The more you invest in them and challenge them to reach their full potential, the more engaged they will become. The scary part of AMA's recent report is that not only are workers not engaged, 15 percent of them are totally disengaged. We have work to do![9]

In *Leveraging Your Leadership Style*, John and I talk about mentoring. AMA is also finding that companies who offer a mentoring program are retaining employees at higher percentages.[10] As employees build relationships with their mentors, they feel more connected to the company on a personal level. Mentoring is all about leading through relationships. Are you seeing the trend here? We are at a crossroads, and what we've done in the past isn't going to work in the future—not if we want to achieve greatness. We cannot look at employees as projects or costs in our business; rather, they **are** the business.

> *We are not primarily put on this earth to see through one another, but to see one another through.*
> —Peter DeVries[11]

Take advantage of this workbook and learn as much about the different personalities as you can. Work on adapting your style so that you can reach more people with ease. Here we go!

CHAPTER THREE
Commanders Get IT Done!

Enough said, right? As Commanders, you naturally want to get results, achieve goals and do it all **fast**. Commanders work at the speed of light, but not everyone else in the world can keep up, thus you can feel frustrated at times with your less-efficient colleagues. I know you are good at whatever you do, but this chapter will help you do it even better. Bottom line, it will help you be more successful by adapting slightly to influence others.

By now, you understand the different leadership/personality styles. I (Lorraine) will now offer some real situations and see if you have captured the essence of approaching people differently. You're a person on the go, so let's jump right in.

Case Study #1: Budget Blues

You have just received news that budgets must be cut. Everyone just burned the midnight oil to get their numbers turned in, and now they must revise them—most likely having to cut in places where it will hurt. Company goals and objectives remain.

On your team, you have a customer service manager who is very supportive of her team and often petitions their feedback before she makes decisions. You also have a very outgoing, positive sales manager who really struggled with the budget because he is more comfortable with relationships than numbers. Your marketing manager is a high achiever who is aggressive and pushes her team hard. Your controller—a very analytical number cruncher—has been instrumental in the process, but nonetheless, he will also be required to slash his budget.

1. Without demoralizing everyone, how do you communicate to the group the change in plans and the need for new numbers?

_____

_____

2. How would you specifically address your customer service manager?

_____

_____

_____

3. Your sales manager?

_____

_____

_____

4. Your marketing manager?

_____

_____

_____

5. Your controller?

_____

_____

_____

The Opportunities

So, did you meet one-on-one or gather the group together for a debriefing session? Both have pros and cons. You'll save time getting everyone together at once, but you may lose the opportunity to specifically target your news to each manager. If you don't already have them, I would encourage you to have weekly one-on-ones with your management team. They don't have to be long, but you can keep on top of things and speak directly to their particular leadership style, which will get you further ahead in the long run.

Your customer service manager is most likely a Counselor. She will be distressed over how her team will be affected by the budget. You will want to address her concerns for her people, which will mean actually slowing down long enough to *hear* her concerns. Encourage her to get her team involved so that it isn't a shock to them. Help her look on the bright side—that the team can pull together on this.

Your sales manager is probably a Coach and will feel overwhelmed if you provide too many details, so keep it simple and to the point at hand, yet don't box him in. Allow creativity here and focus on the end goal, not how he gets there. This will relieve some of the pressure so that he doesn't get "stuck."

Your marketing manager, who is a Commander, will be difficult to slow down enough to discuss the budget; and she probably won't be happy about having to spend more time on it. Emphasize any bonuses associated with working within the new budget parameters and create some challenges for her—doing more with less! If you can tap into her competitive spirit, that will be even better.

Your controller, a Conductor, will want to know specifics. Give your feedback as to what you think should be done in a concise manner and be clear with the deadline without being too forceful. Your controller should be comfortable in this arena.

Case Study #2: Client Case

A major client contacted you directly about his frustration with your company. He came to you first before deciding to take his business elsewhere. In the conversation, you learned that delivery dates had been promised by the sales department but were not met. In addition, he had to call personally for the status update, which means customer service was not proactive. Accounting sent him the bill for a shipment he hadn't even received, and no one in production has returned his call to date.

Your sales manager is a Commander, your customer service manager is a Coach, your accounting manager is a Counselor, and your production manager is a Conductor. When you bring the management team together to discuss this important client, everyone starts pointing fingers and stating, "Well, he said," "She was supposed to," etc.

1. What do you focus on in the meeting? How do you communicate in such a manner that it works for every member of the team without losing the urgency of the situation?

_____

_____

_____

2. What action do you expect of your sales manager, and how do you express it?

_____

_____

_____

3. Of your customer service manager?

_____

_____

_____

4. Of your accounting manager?

_____

_____

_____

5. Of your production manager?

_____

_____

_____

The Solutions

Obviously, you need to make things right for your client. You must first get to the bottom of the situation and learn what really happened. As the leader, your job is to discover what went wrong without assigning blame. Provide an environment that is direct, encouraging, safe, and specific in order to keep each of your managers engaged. When you do, you'll get honesty, not responsibility-dodging.

As you interact with your sales manager, a Commander, be sure to commend his high-energy sales efforts but reinforce the objective, which is ultimately client satisfaction. Stress the goal and ask him how he intends to do things differently in the future to avoid such a situation again.

Your customer service manager, a Coach, will need to know how upset your client really is, and how the relationship has suffered as a result but is not beyond repair. Compliment her on her ability to create rapport with people and encourage her to make things right with the customer. Suggest that she assess all customer relations at the present and perhaps beef up contact in order to increase satisfaction levels, which will make her job easier and more enjoyable.

Your accounting manager, a Counselor, will feel horrible about the error. Turn his energy away from guilt to "how to remedy the situation." Ask some active questions to draw him into a positive solution that he will be eager to implement and to make standard policy for future dealings. Just remember to allow him to speak, which may require a "pause" on your part. Drink some water while you wait!

Last, your production manager, a Conductor, has most likely gotten paralyzed by analysis and is stuck in the numbers or systems of the business. She hasn't lifted her head up to see what is really transpiring around her. Encourage her to meet with her team and get facts and figures on how they are performing, or not performing. Give her a deadline to present you with a solution/system/procedure that will correct this broken link in the chain. Don't push too hard at the initial meeting to get answers. Allow her time to gather her thoughts and get back to you. Then, give her the floor to present her ideas to you at the appropriate time and ask intelligent questions that will help guide her to the right conclusion.

Real Life

In these cases, as it is with life, many more variables exist; but you get the idea that *how* you approach people and situations can set them up for success. Rather than fighting over the words, you are moving ahead to solutions—faster and more effectively!

> *Everything that irritates us about others can lead to an understanding of ourselves.*
>
> —Carl Jung[1]

CHAPTER FOUR
Coaches Make It Fun!

As Coaches, you bring an element of fun wherever you go. Unfortunately, certain aspects of leadership can be difficult, but that doesn't mean it has to be impossible or total drudgery. You are a master at building rapport with people. Couple your natural talents with the understanding you have gained of the different personalities, and you have a recipe for very exciting times! This chapter will help you be more engaging with others and create better teams by adapting your style to influence others.

Observe any team, and you will see every style. The very best television programs use the synergy between the blends. Look at *Seinfeld*: Kramer's high energy is fun and contagious, like you Coaches. Elaine's opinions, strong will, and determination are admirable, like the Commanders. Jerry is always supporting everyone and trying to keep the peace, like Counselors, while George has systems, schedules, and structures for just about everything—even dating (what a Conductor)! The show wouldn't be as lively without the combination of all personalities. It *is* what makes the show.

As a Coach, you might wish that everyone would lighten up a bit, but sometimes the best approach is what works for someone else. I (Lorraine) am going to offer some real situations for you that provide the opportunity to alter your interactions to fit others. Use what you have learned so far and make it fun.

Case Study #1: Breaking Up Is Hard to Do

You are the president of a large ministry organization/nonprofit. You inherited a fellow who is steamrolling over those below him and pushing the buttons of those above him. He is abrasive, controlling, and not living out the mission statement in his role as director. After jumping through all the hoops, crossing your t's and dotting your i's, you come to the conclusion that you must let him go. And by the way, he's the founder's brother-in-law.

1. How do you handle the situation with the founder, who is a Conductor?

_____

_____

_____

2. How do you conduct the exit interview with the director?

_____

_____

_____

3. How do you break the news to the director's secretary, who is a Counselor?

_____

_____

_____

4. The director's fund-raising team consists of three Coaches. How do you communicate the news to them without jeopardizing financial goals?

_____

_____

_____

The Scoop

"Jumping through the hoops" means that you obtained approval for this very delicate matter. But you must still handle the founder with "kid gloves." Facts are facts. They aren't subjective but objective. Diligently gather documentation and notes in your file, along with anything from human resources that they have, and confidently present the situation and why you resolved it the way you did. Remember, the director was hurting the ministry/nonprofit and not adhering to the mission statement. Point out to the founder this disregard for policies and procedures as well as the human impact. He is a man of logic, so as long as you have a solid case, you *should* be fine.

Any matter of this nature can be sticky, but when you communicate in a manner that matches the person's style, you won't add additional sparks to the already hot topic. I know this can be unpleasant and draining for you, but by adapting yourself to the founder, you will ultimately create a friendly environment.

As far as the director goes, you will need to prepare yourself for the attack. If he has blatantly broken rules and steamrolled over people, he will attempt to do the same to you. Chances are, he will be very direct and abrupt. In his mind, he is always right and did nothing wrong. First, I'd encourage you to have a witness—probably someone from HR. Second, do not try to fight with him; you won't stand a chance. Instead, take charge by hitting the bottom line without all the details. Although you might feel better listing all the mistakes he has made, it will only make him hotter. Be direct, firm, to the point, and remember to stick to business all the way. Control your emotions.

Set a time to conduct the exit interview and conclude it on your timetable. Provide the director an opportunity to gather his things. Do try to allow him the dignity of walking out on his own. However, if he gets out of control, then you will need to have security escort him off the premises. Keep in mind at all times, he is still the founder's brother in-law even if he isn't an employee anymore. Be respectful.

You will need to notify his secretary prior to the exit interview. Again, this is another sticky situation. She will feel loyalty to her boss. She must keep this in confidence. The best scenario is to have someone break the news to her while you are conducting the exit interview. Whoever tells her must show compassion for the awkwardness and communicate some plan so that she knows what to expect "tomorrow." Change without all the supporting personal details is difficult for Counselors to swallow. You cannot go into details with her, but you can assure her of future security. Focus on how she can rebuild a steady, safe environment sooner rather than later, and she will handle the transition better.

When you address the director's team, be positive about what they have accomplished together and even praise individuals, if you can, for their efforts. Remind the team that they are talented, gifted, and good at what they do. Be sure to communicate what you know about *who* they will be reporting to, as this is critical to them. Even if you have a temporary arrangement, let them know so that they can focus their energies on doing their jobs rather than wondering who they will be working with.

Intensely negative situations like this one are never fun, but Coaches can have confidence in the fact that extracting the source of negativity to a team will improve the group's experience and effectiveness overall. It is important to realize that even those things that are flat-out painful can be done in a more pleasant way when we use the principles outlined in *Leveraging Your Leadership Style*.

> *The task ahead of us is never as
> great as the Power behind us.*
>
> —*Anonymous*

Case Study #2: Trade Off

The project manager for your company's industry trade show just quit, leaving behind many unfinished details such as confirmation of booth specs and requirements, product and service features, marketing and publicity, sales appointments, and travel arrangements. You were a part of the team but have now been promoted to acting project manager because of your rapport with everyone. You are an encourager but have been tasked with ensuring a successful event. Your team consists of a Commander, Coach, Counselor, and Conductor. You have a month to pull it all together.

1. What is the Commander's strength, what should you delegate to her, and how should you communicate it to her?

_____

_____

_____

2. What is the Coach's strength, what should you delegate to him, and how should you communicate it to him?

_____

_____

_____

3. What is the Counselor's strength, what should you delegate to him, and how should you communicate it to him?

_____

_____

_____

4. What is the Conductor's strength, what should you delegate to her, and how should you communicate it to her?

_____

_____

_____

T-E-A-M

You might feel uncomfortable at first delegating to your peers, but keep in mind that you will all be working as a team. Everyone just needs to pull together to make the trade show happen. And since you all get along, you can have some fun in the process! Communicating it right from the beginning will be the key.

As you assess the workload, look for the difficult challenges that your Commander can go after for you. She will have no difficulty contacting the media at the last minute to arrange some promotion, for instance. The pressure of being behind might actually force her to perform even better. Provide a priority list and let her go! How she does it is up to her.

Consider your fellow Coach for any relationship-oriented aspects of the show such as contacting accounts and arranging sales calls. He will probably have the best relationships, other than you, of anyone on the team and will enjoy the opportunity of talking with people and possibly meeting them at the show. Compliment him on his ability to relate with people and emphasize how important the relationships are to the success of the show, and he will make things happen in a New York minute!

Your Counselor member would be a good fit for something a bit more behind the scenes yet still critical, such as the travel arrangements. He can work on this on his timetable but will have sensitivity to everyone's needs and requests. He might feel under pressure simply because of the urgency of the show, but if you offer some support and proper tools (like the travel budget and the name of the agency the company uses), he will be happy to help.

Conductors love details, so anything that requires streams of paperwork, precision, calculations, and measurements is ideal for them. Your Conductor would be best suited for the booth specs and any unique requirements you have for the show: power plugs, lighting, A/V, and so forth. Be sure to give her the exact deadlines that everything must be done and encourage her to seek help if she gets stuck.

A big event like this will have an array of activities, but with attention to each person's leadership style, you can divvy up the jobs to match everyone's strengths. You can also see that *how* you delegate it can make a world of difference. Everyone can do what they are best at and have fun!

Real Life

In these cases, as it is with life, many more variables exist, but how you approach people and situations can set them up for success. Rather than dodging responsibility or playing the blame game, you are focusing on the heart of the matter and enjoying the process a bit more.

> *The will of God never takes you to where*
> *the grace of God will not protect you.*
>
> —Anonymous

CHAPTER FIVE
Counselors Know Why It Matters

Personally, I thank God for all Counselors. You are others-focused by design, team-oriented naturally, and truly invested in relationships as a way of life. The teams you build tend to be very close and loyal. Your care and concern for others, however, can get in the way when it comes to leadership. The difficult, messy, and stressful aspects of being in charge can be a struggle for you. Thankfully, you have learned that it doesn't mean you aren't a leader, you are just different from Commanders, Coaches, and Conductors. You have your own style—be proud of it! But with any style, we must look at what it takes for us to achieve all-around success. And for Counselors, communication is the key.

Here are some examples of poor communication that were printed and distributed in actual church bulletins:

The Fasting and Prayer Conference includes meals.

The sermon this morning is "Jesus Walks on the Water," and tonight's sermon will be "Searching for Jesus."

Ladies, don't forget the rummage sale. It's a chance to get rid of those things not worth keeping around the house. Bring your husbands.

The peacemaking meeting scheduled for today has been canceled due to a conflict.

Learning how to communicate to each of the different styles will help you feel a bit more comfortable with challenging situations, so I (Lorraine) am providing some case studies for you to review. Take your time with them and see how you might respond in a way that strengthens your leadership, builds your team, and moves you further ahead!

Case Study #1: He Said/She Said

You own a small business where everyone works very closely together. One day, you overhear a heated discussion between two team members. They actually begin to yell at each other, and you feel compelled to step in. You ask Employee A what is going on. Employee A states that she asked Employee B to provide numbers to her by the end of the week so that she could complete a project due by the end of the month.

Before she can finish, Employee B steps in and shouts, "Noooo, you said that two weeks would be fine. I specifically remember telling you that two weeks worked for me and that I would get the numbers to you then."

So upset she is turning red, Employee A bursts into tears and says, "You are lying! You just dropped the ball and don't want to get into trouble. Now I won't be able to deliver my project on time, and it is all your fault!"

Before it gets any worse, you must manage the situation and ask them to step into your office. These two employees have seemed to work well together in the past, but they may have some other issues going on.

1. If Employee A is a Coach, how would you talk her through the issues? How would you seek to resolve the issue and conflict?

_____

_____

_____

2. If Employee A is a Counselor, how would you get her to calm down? How would you seek to resolve the issue and conflict?

_____

_____

_____

3. If Employee B is a Conductor, what would work best in getting him to settle down? How would you seek to resolve the issue and conflict?

_____

_____

_____

4. If Employee B is a Commander, how do you approach him without making matters worse? How would you seek to resolve the issue and conflict?

_____

_____

_____

The Heart of the Matter

Because of your Counselor style, you would know these two employees one-on-one and would have some idea of their personal life as well as how they were handling the pressures of work. With Employee A as a Coach, you wouldn't want to embarrass her in front of her co-worker or disregard her feelings. Instead, you would warmly validate her concerns and extend understanding for how frustrated and upset she must be, without taking sides. Simply relating with her should calm her down; but if it doesn't, ask her to take a deep breath. The next step must be to get the truth from her without the emotion. Coaches can often exaggerate and don't naturally focus on details. Use your relational style with a little extra energy to help her explain the exact due date, what is still required, and how important this project is in the big scope of things. To resolve the situation, you must guide her past "he said/she said" and blaming to finding a positive solution.

If Employee A is a Counselor like you, give her a minute to compose herself. Offer her a tissue and something to drink. Don't rush into getting to the bottom of things, but rather break it up into smaller questions, allowing her time to respond. If she pulls away and gets quiet, ask her if she needs another minute but continue on with the conversation. Again, you will need to get specifics on the project, not the blowup. Coach her past the disagreement and onto ways to make this work. Be sure to determine how critical this project really is as she may have attached a greater value to it than is warranted.

Employee B as a Conductor may be very cold at this point because he feels he is not in the wrong. Details *are* his specialty, you know. However, you must not make this a "right/wrong" scenario, but rather one of finding a resolution. You can jump right into questioning what he has done so far, if anything, and how long it would take him to produce the numbers required. Inquire if anyone else on the team could pick up other tasks to enable him to focus his energies on this particular report. Refrain from being too friendly and soft or he may snap back a bit. If you keep it "strictly business," he will shift gears immediately to the end goal.

And finally, if Employee B is a Commander, do not take anything said personally. On the flip side, do not permit the temper tantrum to continue. That stopped when you asked them both into your office. You are in charge. Be direct but not in his face. Get to the bottom line of what exactly he can provide and when. Petition him for a solution and create a challenge within it to motivate him to tackle the project instead of Employee A!

> *I don't measure a man's success by how high he climbs*
> *but by how high he bounces when he hits bottom.*
> —George S. Patton[1]

Case Study #2: You Don't Say

You have been asked to participate in a business job placement expo. Candidates are seeking employment in leadership positions. You have twenty minutes to share about your company and why it would be an excellent place to work. In the audience, you have Commanders, Coaches, Counselors, and Conductors.

1. How do you capture and retain the Commander's attention? What will they be looking for in your company?

_____

_____

_____

2. How do you interact with the Coaches and keep them engaged? What do they want to know about your company?

_____

_____

_____

3. How do you relate with the Counselors and ensure they feel connected with you? What matters most to them about your company?

_____

_____

_____

4. How do you get the Conductors to listen and stay with you? What questions must you answer for them about your company?

_____

_____

_____

Present with Style

Any time you have a group of people, you will have different styles represented. You must speak to each style in order to win them all over. Simply put, if you make your presentation direct, inspiring, supportive, and detailed, you will meet everyone's needs and will not leave anyone behind.

Commanders are going to want to know what your company can do for them. What positions are available, what objectives or goals does the company have, and what challenges need to be overcome? They love a good challenge! You can be very direct and to the point for them when sharing these specifics.

Coaches will be more concerned with the company's mission statement, the way it develops the team, and the company culture. In a nutshell, share with them some stories of how much fun it can be to work at your company. They are interested in the people side of things. Don't be afraid to be more animated during this part of your presentation—and Coaches love jokes!

Counselors will certainly care about your mission statement, but they will also want to hear more about your values. What is most important to the company, and what type of work environment do you have? Be honest about your company and how it treats its people. Share from your heart, which you do very well.

Conductors want the hard, cold facts about the business. How is the company doing, what is your growth projection, and what are your pay ranges? You cannot possibly address every question they have, so come prepared with literature to hand out to them so they can review it at their leisure. Make sure your information is accurate and correct.

If you weave a little bit of each of these into any presentation, you will reach everyone. I know that this matters to you.

Real Life

Real life has many other variables to consider, of course, but you of all types understand that people's experience of the challenges at hand can impact their success. Rather than avoiding the issues, concentrate on helping others, which is your gift.

> *There is no more noble occupation in the world*
> *than to assist another human being—to help someone succeed.*
> *—Alan Loy McGinnis[2]*

CHAPTER SIX:
Conductors Know What Works

In chapter 2, you read some alarming statistics about how very important it is to lead well and build strong relationships with your team. It is paramount to your long-term success. As a Conductor, you are the master of tasks, but you may not always know what is the "right" thing to do with people because tasks are more concrete and people are ever changing (more like mush!). The good news is that you are learning more and more about how to identify the different styles and what will work for them. Your next step is to now apply it.

I know you appreciate working through things, so I (Lorraine) am providing you a couple of case studies that will allow you to think, digest, and then determine what would be the best approach for the particular situation. You have a natural ability toward correctness, so use it and combine it with your newfound knowledge of the leadership styles.

Case Study #1: Show Your Appreciation

You are the newly appointed director of food services for a mid-size hospital. Your leadership team consists of a certified dietician, head cook, a registered nurse, and the janitorial supervisor. During your on-boarding process, you learn that everyone is on the brink of quitting. The last director was a tyrant, so you are told. No one feels appreciated for all the hard work they do or the stress they endure. Your first objective is to turn things around and retain the leadership team because they have extensive background, experience, and knowledge of the hospital. Besides, they all seem to be doing an outstanding job.

1. Your dietician is a Commander. What do you think she values most (time off, bonuses, etc.) and what can you do immediately to show her appreciation?

_____

_____

2. Your cook is a Coach. What do you think he values most, and what can you do immediately to show him appreciation?

_____

_____

_____

3. Your RN is a Counselor. What do you think he values most, and what can you do immediately to show him appreciation?

_____

_____

_____

4. Your janitorial supervisor is a Conductor, like you. What do you think she values most, and what can you do immediately to show her appreciation?

_____

_____

_____

Different Strokes for Different Folks

As leaders, we must understand our people and what motivates them. Everyone is different. Although we have varying backgrounds, using the leadership style model, you can meet needs based upon their primary mode of operation. For instance, your dietician is a goal-oriented individual. You would want to check when her last raise was as money is often a big motivator for Commanders. If she is underpaid, give her the raise. Her tension will decrease because she will feel respected. If her pay is in an appropriate range, you could provide a gift certificate and then set a performance-based bonus plan for the future. This gives her something to strive for and to focus her energies on. You'll find it easy to stick to business with her. Be careful not to get stuck in the details, though, and keep your pace moving along.

Your cook could probably use some cheerleading from you, which isn't the first place you go, but you can do it. Coaches seek approval and praise. He's probably sick of being around hot food and constant time pressures. Something to consider would be a lunch out with him alone. You haven't observed his work personally, but you can share your gratitude for keeping things going smoothly, doing well on performance issues, etc. Do some homework on his department to feel adequately prepared. Sing all the praises you can as he enjoys recognition. Be sure to give him sincere compliments in the presence of others when you can.

Your RN is probably exhausted and hasn't told a soul. Counselors will take a lot, but can finally snap without warning. To head this off at the pass, sit down with him and simply ask how he is doing. He may not immediately answer, or he might feel uncomfortable, so ask what he needs. Does he need a vacation? Does he need more personnel? How is he doing with resources? Then listen. Allow him time to tell how he is doing and to talk with you. Be patient and kind. Consider the person not the task, and you will win him over. Continued support can be provided to him with thank-you cards. These go a very long way, so don't underestimate their power.

Your janitorial supervisor will be the easiest team member to meet with because she is a Conductor like you. You can ask questions about specific job duties and how they are going, knowing that you will receive "just the facts." You would probably give your janitor advance notice to come to the meeting prepared with issues that you could help her with. Working through these together would energize her—and you! Look at ways to improve systems, schedules, etc. She will enjoy it and feel appreciated when you accept her plans.

The basic cause of most inharmonious human relationships is the tendency to impose our values on other people.
—*Robert Anthony*[1]

Case Study #2: Let's Work Together

You have volunteered to help bring a satellite-training program to your church. You have been deemed team leader and will be responsible for scheduling meetings with four individuals who are all volunteers as well. You will be in charge of ensuring that their respective areas are on target for the event date, which is in three months. Everyone has received their directives and has lay staff working under them.

1. Your fund raiser is constantly late for all the meetings, arriving in a whirl of activity. She is high energy and apologizes for always being late. She smiles as she shares her great story as to why she was late. What is her dominant style? How can you best communicate with her? How can you keep her on track?

_____

_____

_____

_____

_____

2. Your marketing and PR person attends meetings but does not give you his full attention. He is either receiving telephone calls or making them during the meetings. He indicates to keep pressing on because he has limited time. He often has to leave early. What is his dominant style? How can you best communicate with him? How can you keep him on track?

_____

_____

_____

_____

_____

3. Your facilities guy arrives early, greets you, and then sits down without saying much. He is neat and very organized, bringing his planner to every meeting. He takes incredible notes. What is his dominant style? How can you best communicate with him? How can you keep him on track?

_____

_____

_____

_____

4. Your event planner, who will handle the meals and decorations, is a sweet gal. She has a warm smile and has compliments for everyone in the room. She is the one who asks if anyone needs anything before the meeting begins. What is her dominant style? How can you best communicate with her? How can you keep her on track?

_____

_____

_____

_____

Doing What Is Right

First of all, no matter who we are, we need to acknowledge that everyone else is not like us. As Conductors, you may struggle with the different styles a bit more, especially the Coaches and Commanders. They can appear improper or brash compared to your measures. However, your team—your life—requires _everyone_ to bring balance. Without all the styles, the world would be a scary place. So, relax a bit and extend grace. Your fund-raiser, although she isn't prompt, has the gift of gab. As a Coach, she is the perfect person for getting out into the community and building excitement about the event. In addition, she is probably well connected and will get those donations you need so that you can stay within budget. Don't sweat the small stuff, and concentrate on keeping the energy positive and providing her places to use her gift. Bring a list of potential vendors and donors so that she can do her magic. Do set a time that she must have everything in to you, and follow up. Don't wait for her to get back to you.

Your marketing and PR man is a mover and shaker. Even though Commanders can come across as rude and annoying, try not to set too many rules on them. Focus on the end results, which is what he will be doing. However, agreeing to dedicate a certain amount of the meeting to go over details uninterrupted is essential. Create an agenda for every meeting and email it in advance so that everyone can be prepared. Put this guy up first so he can report and leave if he has to. As long as he has his marching orders, he will get it done. He's goal oriented and wants to succeed.

Your facilities guy will be right there with you as he is a Conductor too. He most likely will turn in a grid he created with all his duties, team assignments, required resources, and due dates. Each meeting, he will update you with specific details on how the room setup is going, on the progress of the lighting and sound crew, etc. Just as you can get stuck in analyzing and processing, be sure he is moving through to action. If something needs to be researched, set a deadline for it and then make a decision. As the leader, you need to keep this moving along.

Finally, your event planner has a heart of gold and is ideal for addressing all the little things that make an event memorable and enjoyable. As a Counselor, she will be thinking of others, so look out for her. Watch for signs of stress, which are withdrawing, retreating, not responding, etc. At each meeting, ask her how *she* is doing so that you keep your connection strong. If anything for the event changes, let her know immediately and help her understand why so she can change her course smoothly. Try not to dump any last-minute changes on her if you can avoid it.

Real Life

As you well know, there are more details to consider than could ever be covered here, but the bottom line is that by knowing and addressing the specific needs of each person's style, you can help lead them to success. Rather than processing just the details and tasks, you can involve the people, increasing your chances of getting the job done right the first time.

> *The way we communicate with others and with ourselves*
> *ultimately determines the quality of our lives.*
> —*Anthony Robbins,* Unlimited Power[2]

CHAPTER SEVEN
Total Quality Leadership

By this point, after reading the book and working through this workbook, you have substantially increased your leadership capacity. Remember our definition: Leadership is influence in the context of positive and proactive relationships. So by now, our hope is that you:

- Know your own leadership style
- Know the leadership style of your primary team members
- Have thought about and practiced effective communication, challenged your team members to leverage their own leadership styles, and experienced conflict resolution with the various leadership styles represented on your team
- Have grown to appreciate the gifts that the various styles bring to the party

All Together Now

In the following exercises, I want to help you to bring it all together so that you can practice Total Quality Leadership. We'll identify your core strengths once again, think about how you can best influence others in the context of positive and proactive relationships, and determine how you can shore up your weaknesses.

1. Which leadership style best represents you? Are you a Commander, Coach, Counselor, or Conductor? Remember, most people have a primary style and a secondary style—which is your *primary* style and which is your *secondary* style?

_____

_____

_____

2. When people "love" working with you, what aspects of your leadership style are most often talked about? When people "hate" working with you, what aspects of your leadership style are most often talked about?

_____

_____

_____

3. What are the primary and secondary leadership styles of your team members? List their names and both their primary and secondary leadership styles here:

TEAM MEMBER NAME	PRIMARY LEADERSHIP STYLE	SECONDARY LEADERSHIP STYLE

4. When your team is operating at the very best (positively and proactively), how would you describe the environment and relationships between the team members?

_____

As you operate out of your core philosophy that positive and proactive relationships are the way to influence people toward their highest and greatest personal fulfillment and simultaneously maximize their contributions to the organization, you are well on your way to Total Quality Leadership! This all may seem like a bit of a balancing act—if you are thinking that, you are in good company! I (John) have been in leadership roles for close to thirty years now, and I don't think I've ever gotten it completely right. Leading an organization can be a little bit like directing a musical production that always feels like it is at dress rehearsal stage. Jan Carzon of the Scandinavian Air System went so far as to say: "All business is show business." We agree. All business is show business. All leadership is show business. All management is show business. That doesn't mean tap dancing, it means shaping your team's values and inspiring action, as a powerful play might affect an audience. It is the opposite of administration and, especially, "professional management."[1] What you "produce" in leadership is the outgrowth of the relationships you build between team members and the way that action is translated from the symbols and focus you create.

5. Clarity in leadership is essential. What are the key values that you want to shape in your teams and organization? If you are successful in shaping those key values, what will be the resulting actions?

Part of the putting it all together is to recognize that, at heart, *Leveraging Your Leadership Style* is all about managing your own leadership with regard to your relationships with others. In their book *The Service Profit Chain*, James Heskett, W. Earl Sasser, and Leonard Schlesinger make the case that no matter what your business, the only way to generate enduring profits is to begin by building the kind of work environment that attracts, focuses, and keeps talented employees.[2] We agree with their focus on personal development and in recognizing that the leadership role is all about "calling forth" the gifts, strengths, and potential of those you work with.

Effective leaders recognize the opportunity they have to call forth the gifts and talents of others. Throughout *Leveraging Your Leadership Style*, we have encouraged you to recognize the strengths not only in your style but in the styles of others. Alan Nelson, a friend and colleague of mine (John), is the current editor of *Rev! Magazine*. I agree with Alan when he says, "Leadership is a social relationship in which people allow individuals to influence them toward intentional change. Leadership involves more than leaders and what they do. Power ultimately resides in the followers or collaborators."[3] Leaders who are leveraging their leadership style will be working on the strengths of their leadership in partnership with their team members.

6. In what ways have you solicited and received help from your team members? Think of someone on your team who has a different leadership style from yours. How have you come to appreciate his or her unique perspectives and strengths?

_____

_____

_____

7. Consider the makeup of your current team. How are your team members strong in the areas where you are weak? What specific ways does this benefit you? List the areas of their strengths and how they are most complementary to your weaknesses.

_____

_____

_____

Evaluating Ourselves

Recently, our organization has been undergoing substantial transition with several members being moved out of our current team. During this period of time, I (John) have been looking at my own strengths and weaknesses and have been talking with team members about what makes our team healthy and what areas continue to need work. In that process, I've gone back to what I consider the key elements of Total Quality Leadership. I thought it might be helpful to consider those here.

1. Leaders **cast vision**. How can you elevate your team to consider what great future might be theirs if you accomplish your vision?

_____

_____

_____

2. Leaders **create environments**. How can you create contexts where your team can experience health and growth at personal and corporate levels?

_____

_____

_____

3. Leaders **develop systems**. What procedures and processes could you use to ensure consistency and stability in your organization?

_____

_____

_____

4. Leaders **equip other leaders**. How can you help your team members reproduce the health that they are experiencing on your team?

_____

_____

_____

    I believe in your ability to grow and develop your team! Part of what you do as a leader is to inspire your team to greatness. Regardless of your leadership style, you have the ability to lift your team to higher heights than have been previously experienced. Your Total Quality Leadership *will* make the difference. Go for greatness!

    It's said that Abraham Lincoln often slipped out of the White House on Wednesday evenings to listen to the sermons of Dr. Finnes Gurley at New York Avenue Presbyterian Church. He generally preferred to come and go unnoticed. So when Dr. Gurley knew the President was coming, he left his study door open. On one of those occasions, the President slipped through a side door in the church and took a seat in the minister's study, located just to the side of the sanctuary. There he propped the door open, just wide enough to hear Dr. Gurley. During the walk home, an aide asked Mr. Lincoln his appraisal of the sermon. The President thoughtfully replied, "The content was excellent; he delivered with elegance; he obviously put work into the message." "Then you thought it was an excellent sermon?" questioned the aide. "No," Lincoln answered. "But you said that the content was excellent. It was delivered with eloquence, and it showed how hard he worked," the aide pressed. "That's true," Lincoln said, "But Dr. Gurley forgot the most important ingredient. He forgot to ask us to do something great."[4]

—Unknown

CHAPTER EIGHT
Leadership Quotient

W e have been curious and intrigued about a person's Intelligence Quotient (IQ) since the German psychologist William Stern first coined the phrase in 1912.[1] IQ has typically been used by social sciences as an attempt to measure one's intelligence. Almost as old but not as well known is the Emotional Quotient (EQ) used to "describe an ability, capacity, or skill to perceive, assess, and manage the emotions of one's self, of others, and of groups."[2] Perhaps because I (Lorraine) am not a genius, I haven't given much weight to the IQ measurement when it comes to finding and hiring talent. When I think of high IQ, I envision a brilliant but absent-minded professor like "Doc" Brown in the movie, *Back to the Future*! If you are a high IQ person, please don't take offense. I'm just jealous!

The EQ has certainly caught my attention, though, not as the end-all-be-all determining factor but as yet another area to explore when looking for the right people for the right seats on the right bus (thinking about the metaphor Jim Collins uses in *Good to Great*). EQ assesses areas like maturity, social interface, emotions, self-awareness, empathy, etc. In my opinion, IQ is how our mind works and EQ is how we interact in the world or apply what we know.

Judy Fox Brandt, consultant for Fox & Company, states that IQ or internal processes account for roughly 25 percent of a person's success and basically gets you through school. EQ, or behavior, on the other hand, gets you through life and represents about 66 percent of your success. Whew. I'm grateful for that! And, EQ can be improved, but your IQ remains relatively the same through the course of your life. I believe our Leadership Quotient (LQ) is similar. We can grow into tremendous leaders, even if we didn't start that way.

Leadership Intelligence

LQ is what we have been talking about in *Leveraging Your Leadership Style*. It is the ability to adapt one's self to others, which requires being self- *and* others-aware. LQ is what sets us apart from mediocre, average, and trend-following leaders. LQ is leading like Jesus, truly striving for a balanced and appropriate approach to every interaction.

The more you understand yourself and others and then apply that understanding to each situation, the more you are increasing your LQ. The case studies you worked through in this book are perfect examples of beefing up those muscles. The body is an amazing thing. It is designed with everything we need; yet, unless we tap into it, take care of it, and challenge it, it will never reach its full potential. Remember John and I stating early on that we believe God has given each of us the ability to lead? Some people have really worked to develop this ability while others may not have; thus, we have some dynamic, powerful leaders and others that are not yet fully developed. The good news is that, just like physical fitness, it is never too late to improve! We can change our bodies by exercising and eating right, and we can become phenomenal leaders, just as God intended, by working on our LQ.

Put It to the Test

As I (Lorraine) said, the best way to get better is to practice. This has been an interactive book, so let's explore some areas of your LQ and see how you are doing:

1. When confronted with a conflict, do you
    A. Get excited and ready to fight?
    B. Strategically plan how you will win at any cost?
    C. Run in the other direction?
    D. Seek to understand what the underlying issue is and how to resolve the conflict in a manner that will support all parties?
2. As you interact with others, do you
    A. Expect them to read your mind?
    B. Try to adapt your communication and leadership style to better work for them?
    C. Demand that they cater to you?
    D. Passively go with the flow?
3. When delegating to others, do you
    A. Focus on the end result, allowing each individual to accomplish the task as he or she sees fit?
    B. Tell them exactly how it needs to be done?

     C. You don't delegate! You do it yourself because no one can be trusted.

     D. Hope that things will go well but don't check in?

4. When you have to deliver unpleasant news to the troops, do you

     A. Gather everyone together and communicate in a manner that reaches all parties, being as honest as you can?

     B. Stick your head in the sand and wait until it blows over?

     C. Send an email with the details rather than see everyone face to face?

     D. Tell one person and ask them to forward along the message for you?

5. When you are given praise from the top on a project that required your entire team, do you

     A. Take all the credit?

     B. Defer all the credit to your team?

     C. Say you don't deserve the praise?

     D. Graciously accept the praise for you and your team because it was everyone who made it possible.?

Take It to the Next Level

The answers to these questions may seem obvious—or they may not. We are all at different stages of our leadership journey, and we all have room to grow. I hope that these at least made you start thinking about your LQ.

For the first question, anytime we seek to understand first, we are pausing long enough to evaluate what is really happening. When we do that, we will respond much more appropriately. This is effective in personal relationships too.

For the second question, we may feel that others should be speaking our language since we are in the position of leadership, but the reality is that great leaders think of others. We shouldn't make the focus "us"; instead, it should be about influencing, empowering, engaging, motivating, and inspiring others.

For the third question, sometimes we find it easier to just tell people what to do and how to do it, but that doesn't take us to the next level of leadership. When we can allow people to be individuals and to focus on the end results, then we are leading instead of "managing." True delegation gives the person the chance to be creative with *how* they accomplish the task that has been clearly defined.

For the fourth question, just remember that if you don't clearly and directly communicate what is going on, people will make up their own story. And trust me, what their imaginations create will be way worse than the truth because we have all watched too much television! Seriously, you never go wrong with shooting straight with people. Combine honesty with your ability to adapt to the different styles, and you will have enhanced relationships due to improved communication.

For the last question, don't let your ego get in the way. We all have it; in fact, in order to be successful, you'd better be using it. But, it has its place. When it comes to praise and compliments for a job well done, don't forget that you are the quarterback. You are only as good as the players on your team.

> *No program is possible without change.*
> *To achieve the Total Quality Life, you must surrender*
> *what you are for what you will become.*
> —*Stan Toler*[3]

CONCLUSION
Maximize Your Influence

You are a leader! You are exercising influence in your life on a regular basis as you are engaged in positive and proactive relationships. Because you have taken the time to think through your leadership style and the leadership style of your team members, you are well on your way to leveraging *your* leadership style! Your team members will be thankful for your initiative to enhance your leadership and for your appreciation of their leadership styles. You've invested in your team and helped them develop their self-understanding and skills. You've leveraged your total team capacity.

I played tennis in high school and have played periodically since then. In the middle of the tennis racket is what we call the "sweet spot" where we can maximize our effectiveness with efficiency. That sweet spot is where the greatest impact is made with the least effort. Once you are authentically living out the principles in the *Leveraging Your Leadership Style* book and workbook, you and your team will operate in the "sweet spot" of effectiveness. I'm trusting that the sweet spot of your leadership will be a place of fantastic fulfillment. In my own personal experience, when I am operating in the "sweet spot" of my life and leadership, I feel fulfilled even when I am tired —and you will too.

Your capacity for leadership is directly proportional to your ability and willingness to understand and expand the capacities of others and to develop your team together. My prayer and hope has been that you will enjoy the journey of being a leader, and that it will become far more natural to you than ever before. Soon, leadership will "flow" from you organically rather than mechanically through your position or the power of your role.

Truthfully, you are on a leadership journey right now. You read the book and now you have completed the workbook. Whether you are a Commander, a Coach, a Counselor, or a Conductor, you are taking a "road trip" of sorts. You have gone many miles and have learned who is in the car with you! Our prayer for your journey has been that you understand your strengths and your teammates' strengths, and that you desire to help them better leverage their individual strengths. I'll bet you'll never look at a road trip quite the same way! We are even trusting that your family road trip vacations will take on a new meaning, and be even more enjoyable than before!

Leveraging Your Leadership Style is about becoming all that you were meant to be and coaching others to do the same. I hope we've been able to assist you in the journey. Know that the results that come from your leadership efforts will always be leveraged when you are positive and proactive in the context of relationships that work!

Dr. John Jackson

Like John, I am an avid tennis fan. As I am finishing up this workbook, the World Team Tennis championship is being televised. As I was watching the other day, I noticed how fun the environment of WTT is compared to the sterile, stoic one at Wimbledon. People actually cheer and scream. They even play music when a superb point is made! One of the big differences I saw was that the players were smiling and enjoying the process a bit more and taking themselves a little less seriously. Yet they were still giving 100 percent and playing to win, and since WTT is about the team, everyone was playing together toward a common goal.

I personally love playing singles; but as I have gotten older, I am not out to destroy my opponent but rather to give my best. My focus is more on my contribution and not just the victory. I'm a more mature player now, concentrating on strategy and execution rather than sheer willpower and speed. And, people matter. In my youth, the other side of the court was "the enemy." Today, I want the other player to have a good experience and to be able to play his or her best. Although I'm not a WTT star, this changed mindset is helping me settle into a more satisfying tennis career of my own.

As you get in a groove with your leadership style, my hope for you is that you play the game for the benefit of all involved, and actually enjoy the journey of life and leadership. With more tools on your belt, coupled with a greater awareness of others, you should be feeling better equipped to lead no matter where you are and what your title or role. This doesn't mean that life won't throw you some curve balls, but you will have more skill and heart to face them. Yes, heart. Throughout our time together, I hope you have come to appreciate the importance of caring for those you lead. I know it comes easier for those who are Coaches and Counselors.

However, if we are truly going to be better leaders than some of the recent examples in the media, we must care. Trust me, Commanders and Conductors, you will receive major blessings for your efforts—here on earth and in Heaven! We have to take our leadership the extra step and let those we lead *know* how much we care. Understanding and applying the leadership styles is a perfect way to do that.

This workbook gave you some things to think about, process, and consider. Anytime we take a new skill or knowledge and practice applying it to such things as the case studies in chapters 3 through 6, we have dramatically increased our chances of assimilating it into our daily practice. Now start using it in life. In every situation you practice adapting yourself to others, you will become stronger and better. The exciting part is that things will start going more smoothly and more easily because you are building bridges, not creating barriers.

Life is too short. Not a single one of us gets out of it alive. The more time we spend enriching others, the more blessed we become. Leadership is an awesome avenue for making a difference in the lives of others and having an influence upon them. That brings us full circle.

I pray that your influence multiplies. As you share what you know with others, we can all start to create a more harmonious, empowering, respectful, loving, and productive world. We'll have you to thank! Blessings.

Lorraine Bossé-Smith

NOTES

1. Building Bridges

1. Marcus Buckingham and Curt Coffman, *First Break All the Rules* (New York: Simon & Schuster, 1999), 85.

2. Create Stronger Relationships

1. Jay Jamrog, "The Perfect Storm," AMA Business Brief (American Management Association, adapted from *The Perfect Storm: The Future of Retention and Engagement* by Jay Jamrog © 2004, Human Resources Institute, St. Petersburg, Florida), 3.

2. Ibid.

3. John Maxwell, *The Influential Leader*. Live Simulcast, Cornerstone Community Church; Wildomar, CA, April 2004.

4. Jamrog, "The Perfect Storm," 3.

5. Judith Glaser, "The New Leader," *Leadership Excellence* 24, no. 4 (April 2007), 8.

6. Maxwell, *The Influential Leader*.

7. Ibid.

8. Glenn van Ekern, *The Speaker's Sourcebook II*. (Englewood Cliffs, NJ: Prentice Hall, 1994), 223.

9. Jamrog, "The Perfect Storm," 3.

10. Ibid., 7.

11. *The Speaker's Sourcebook II*, 318.

3. Commanders Get IT Done!

1. *The Speaker's Sourcebook II*, 361.

5. Counselors Know Why It Matters

1. George S. Patton, *Do Not Say: "I Have Done Enough."* E-letter edited by Ken Keller with Renaissance Executive Forums, July 5, 2007, 1).

2. *The Speaker's Sourcebook II*, 122.

6. Conductors Know What Works

1. *The Speaker's Sourcebook II*, 317.
2. Ibid., 71.

7. Total Quality Leadership

1. Tom Peters and Nancy Austin, *A Passion for Excellence* (New York: Warner Books, 1985), 311.
2. Buckingham and Coffman, *First, Break All The Rules*, 21.
3. Alan Nelson, *Spirituality & Leadership: Harnessing the Wisdom, Guidance, and Power of the Soul* (Colorado Springs: NavPress Publishing Group, 2002), 23.
4. Ken Blanchard and Jesse Stoner, *Full Steam Ahead: Unleash the Power of Vision in Your Company and Your Life* (San Francisco: Berrett-Koehler Publishers, 2003), 6-7.

8. Leadership Quotient

1. http://en.wikipedia.org/wiki/Intelligence_quotient.
2. http://en.wikipedia.org/wiki/Emotional_intelligence.
3. Stan Toler, *Total Quality Life: Strategies for Purposeful Living* (Indianapolis: Wesleyan Publishing House, 2007), 115.

BIBLIOGRAPHY

Blanchard, Ken, and Jesse Stoner, *Full Steam Ahead: Unleash the Power of Vision in Your Company and Your Life*. San Francisco: Berrett-Koehler Publishers, 2003.

Buckingham, Marcus, and Curt Coffman, *First, Break All the Rules*. New York: Simon & Schuster, 1999.

Church Bulletins – Anonymous Email – April 6, 2007.

Fox Brandt, Judy. *Emotional Intelligence: What It Is and Why It Matters to Your Business*. Presentation made to Executive Forums on June 13, 2007, Rancho Cucamonga, Calif.

Glaser, Judith. "The New Leader: Go From Dictating to Developing," *Leadership Excellence* 24, no. 4 (April 2007).

http://en.wikipedia.org/wiki/Emotional_intelligence, accessed on July 23, 2007.

http://www.wikipedia.org/wiki/Intelligence_quotient, accessed on July 23, 2007.

Jackson, John. *PastorPreneur*. Carson City, NV. VisionQuest Ministries, 2003.

Jamrog, Jay J. *The Perfect Storm: The Future of Retention and Engagement*. St. Petersburg, Fla.: Human Resource Institute, 2004 (adapted version at www.AMAnet.org)

Kawasaki, Guy. *How to Change The World* (Blog).

Maxwell, John. *The Influential Leader*. Live simulcast, Cornerstone Community Church; Wildomar, Calif., April 2004.

Nelson, Alan. *Spirituality & Leadership: Harnessing the Wisdom, Guidance, and Power of the Soul*. Colorado Springs: NavPress Publishing Group, 2002.

Patton, George S. *Do Not Say: "I Have Done Enough."* E-letter edited by Ken Keller with Renaissance Executive Forums, July 5, 2007.

Peters, Tom, and Nancy Austin. *A Passion for Excellence*. New York: Warner Books, 1985.

Sanborn, Mark. *The Fred Factor*. New York: Doubleday Books, 2004.

Sanders, Tim. *The Likeability Factor*. New York: Crown, 2005.

Toler, Stan. *Total Quality Life: Strategies for Purposeful Living*. Indianapolis, Ind.: Wesleyan Publishing House, 2007.

van Ekern, Glenn. *The Speaker's Sourcebook II*. Englewood Cliffs, N.J.: Prentice Hall, 1994.